✦A STEP INTO HISTORY™✦

THE CIVIL WAR

BY STEVEN OTFINOSKI

Series Editor

Elliott Rebhun, Editor & Publisher,

The New York Times Upfront

at Scholastic

■ SCHOLASTIC

Content Consultant: James Marten, PhD, Professor and Chair, History
Department, Marquette University, Milwaukee, Wisconsin

Cover: Soldiers stand near a cannon during the Civil War.

Library of Congress Cataloging-in-Publication Data
Names: Otfinoski, Steven, author.
Title: The Civil War / by Steven Otfinoski.
Description: New York, NY : Children's Press, an imprint of Scholastic Inc., 2017.
 | Series: A step into history | Includes bibliographical references and index.
Identifiers: LCCN 2016031160| ISBN 9780531225691 (library binding) | ISBN
 9780531243633 (paperback)
Subjects: LCSH: United States—History—Civil War, 1861–1865—Juvenile
 literature. | United States—History—Civil War, 1861–1865—Social
 aspects—Juvenile literature. | United States—History—Civil War,
 1861–1865—Influence—Juvenile literature.
Classification: LCC E468 .O75 2017 | DDC 973.7—dc23
LC record available at https://lccn.loc.gov/2016031160

 2 3 4 5 6 7 8 9 10 R 26 25 24 23 22 21 20 19 18

CONTENTS

PROLOGUE

HE CIVIL WAR WAS UNLIKE ANY OTHER war the United States has fought. It was the first and only war where Americans fought one another. The very foundation of the nation hung in the balance. It remains the most defining event in American history, pitting friends against friends and family members against family members.

The elements that caused the war were set in place long before the fighting began. By the early 1800s, the Northern states began to move slowly but steadily from an agricultural economy to an industrial one. The Southern states, on the other hand, remained largely agricultural and rural, with many small farms and large plantations. Much of the Southern economy relied on slave labor.

Slavery had been widespread in the United States for more than 200 years. Beginning in the early 1600s, people in Africa had been captured, loaded onto American and European merchant ships, and brought to America to be sold as slaves. The plantations of the South relied heavily on slave labor to plant and pick cotton, tobacco, and sugar. By 1800, there were nearly 894,000 slaves in the

United States, almost all of them in the South. By this time, slavery had largely disappeared in the North, where many people opposed slavery as morally wrong. Tensions over slavery and its extension into new territories sparked the Civil War, which would last four long years. The war ended in 1865, but many of the issues and feelings it raised are still a part of our lives today.

Drums carried by soldiers from New York, Vermont, and Massachusetts during the Civil War

THE TWO SIDES IN THE CIVIL WAR

THE UNION

25 States

CALIFORNIA

CONNECTICUT

DELAWARE

ILLINOIS

INDIANA

IOWA

KANSAS

KENTUCKY

MAINE

MARYLAND

MASSACHUSETTS

MICHIGAN

MINNESOTA

MISSOURI

NEVADA*

NEW HAMPSHIRE

NEW JERSEY

NEW YORK

OHIO

OREGON

PENNSYLVANIA

RHODE ISLAND

VERMONT

WEST VIRGINIA*

WISCONSIN

6 Territories

COLORADO

DAKOTA

NEBRASKA

NEW MEXICO

UTAH

WASHINGTON

These two states were admitted into the Union during the Civil War.

THE CONFEDERATE STATES OF AMERICA

SOUTH CAROLINA
(December 20, 1860) ←

Dates in parentheses
show when each state
seceded from the Union.

MISSISSIPPI
(January 9, 1861)

FLORIDA
(January 10, 1861)

ALABAMA
(January 11, 1861)

GEORGIA
(January 19, 1861)

LOUISIANA
(January 26, 1861)

TEXAS
(February 1, 1861)

VIRGINIA
(April 17, 1861)

ARKANSAS
(May 6, 1861)

NORTH CAROLINA
(May 20, 1861)

TENNESSEE
(June 8, 1861)

MAPS

A NATION DIVIDED: 1861–1865

During the Civil War, the United States was divided into two main sides: the Union in the North and the Confederacy in the South. There were also five "border states," slave states that remained in the Union.

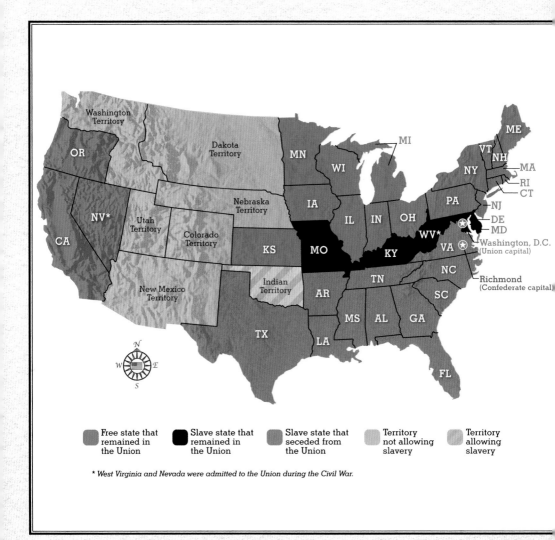

Washington Territory

OR

Dakota Territory

MN

MI

ME

VT

NH

MA

NY

RI

CT

WI

IA

PA

NJ

NV*

Utah Territory

Nebraska Territory

IL IN OH

DE

MD

CA

Colorado Territory

KS

MO

KY

WV*

VA ✪

Washington, D.C.
(Union capital)

New Mexico Territory

Indian Territory

AR

TN

NC

SC

Richmond
(Confederate capital)

MS AL GA

TX

LA

FL

Free state that remained in the Union

Slave state that remained in the Union

Slave state that seceded from the Union

Territory not allowing slavery

Territory allowing slavery

West Virginia and Nevada were admitted to the Union during the Civil War.

MAJOR BATTLES

Most fighting during the Civil War took place in the South, on Confederate soil. A number of major battles were fought at sea, where the Union effectively blocked Confederate access to supplies shipped from Europe.

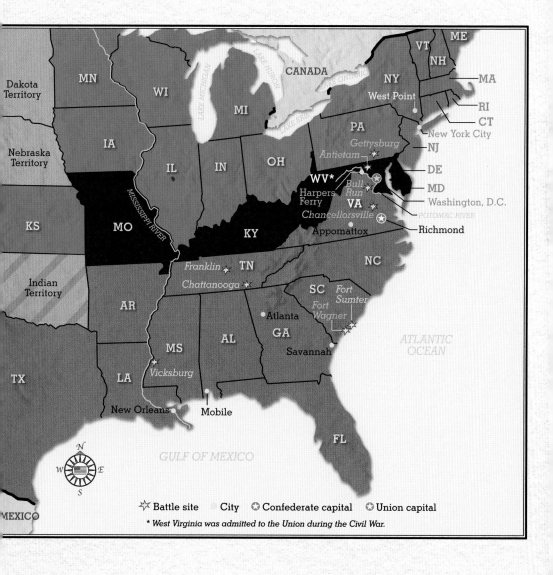

*An enslaved brother
and sister in 1864*

CHAPTER 1

SLAVERY IN AMERICA

America was built on freedom,

but not for everyone.

Slavery was already common in the Caribbean and Latin America.

IN 1619, A DUTCH SHIP BROUGHT 20 ENSLAVED African men to Jamestown, Virginia. This marked the beginning of slavery in North America. Africans were captured, sold to slavers, and shipped to America. There, they lived under horrible conditions. They were forced to do hard work for long hours and no pay. Many slave owners whipped or beat them for the slightest of reasons. Often, enslaved families were broken up when children or parents were sold to another owner. Slavery became an important part of the American economy, especially in the South. Large farms called plantations relied on slave labor to produce tobacco and cotton.

During the 1800s, the North started to become more **industrialized**. Northern factories needed skilled laborers and mechanics. There was, as well, a growing feeling in the North that it was morally wrong for one human being to own another. For these reasons, slavery was in the process of being **abolished** in all the Northern states by 1804. But some Northerners wanted to see slavery abolished across America. These people were called abolitionists.

You will find the definitions of bold words in the glossary on pages 140–41.

Slave owners often punished enslaved people by whipping them. These brutal beatings often left scars.

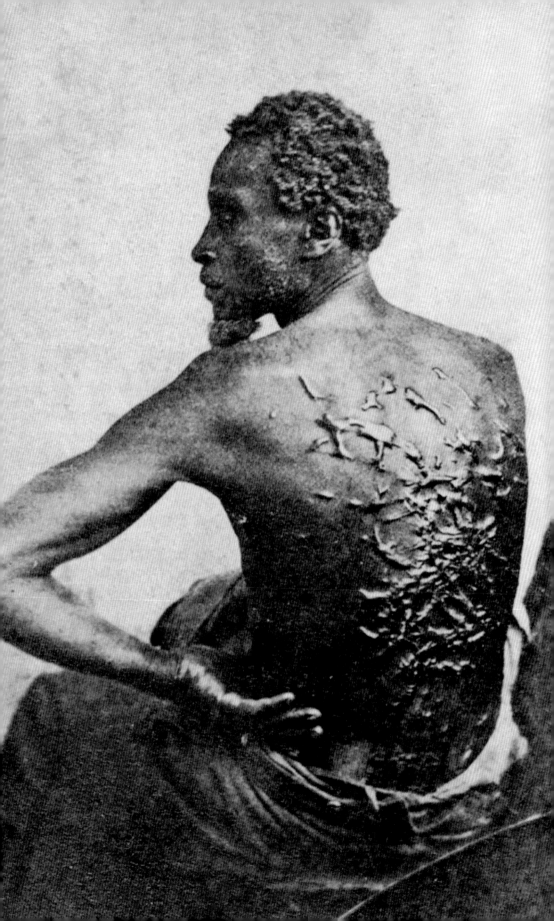

*A U.S. flag dating to
the Civil War era*

CHAPTER 2

A NATION DIVIDED

Slavery and states' rights drove a wedge
between North and South.

BY THE EARLY 1800s, THOUSANDS OF Americans were moving west in search of land and new opportunities. As these pioneers settled new territories, they applied for statehood. This complicated the slavery issue. Slave supporters wanted to allow slavery in these new territories and states. However, many Northerners wanted to confine slavery to the South.

In the 1850s, abolitionists such as Harriet Tubman, Levi Coffin, and many others helped runaway slaves escape the South through the Underground Railroad. This was a system of safe houses where fugitive slaves could hide as they headed north to freedom. Some abolitionists were not satisfied with simply helping slaves escape. John Brown was one of them. He wanted to end slavery by starting a slave **insurrection**. In October 1859, he and a small band of followers tried to seize the federal **arsenal** at Harpers Ferry, Virginia. Brown intended to give the arsenal's weapons to slaves so they could fight their masters. However, the Marines moved in and captured him. Brown was tried for treason and hanged. Abolitionists hailed him as a hero, while the South condemned him as a criminal. The nation was more divided than ever.

Many slaves also escaped on their own, without help from abolitionists.

John Brown walks down the stairs on the way to his execution in 1859.

John Brown had led several attacks against slavery supporters before his raid on Harpers Ferry.

" A house divided against itself cannot stand. I believe this government cannot endure permanently half slave and half free. "

—ABRAHAM LINCOLN, JUNE 16, 1858

CHAPTER 3

ABRAHAM LINCOLN FOR PRESIDENT

The Republican presidential candidate came from humble beginnings. He would become one of our greatest leaders.

Find out more about people whose names appear in orange and bold on pages 134-35.

A T THE TIME, ONE OF THE MOST OUTSPOKEN politicians on the slavery issue was Abraham Lincoln. Lincoln had been born and raised in the backwoods of Kentucky and Indiana, where he received less than a year of formal schooling. He had a good mind, however, and worked hard to become a lawyer.

At age 25, Lincoln entered politics. He served in the Illinois House of Representatives from 1834 to 1842 and the U.S. House of Representatives from 1847 to 1849. He ran twice to be a U.S. senator from Illinois (1854 and 1858) and lost both times. The second time, he ran against Stephen Douglas. In a series of debates against Douglas, Lincoln opposed extending slavery into the territories. He called it "a moral, social, and political evil." However, he was not an abolitionist. He was willing to allow slavery to continue in the South in order to preserve the Union.

Though Lincoln lost the Senate elections, the debates made him famous. Two years later, in 1860, the recently formed Republican Party chose him to be its candidate for president.

Abraham Lincoln poses for a photo soon after becoming president in 1861.

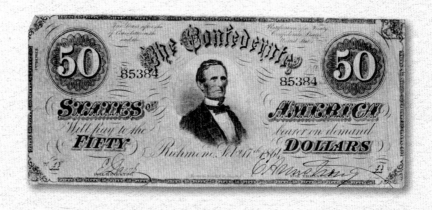

Currency used by the Confederate
states during the war

CHAPTER 4

SECESSION

Lincoln entered office
facing a daunting challenge.

You will find the dates that each Confederate state seceded on page 11.

I N 1860, LINCOLN DEFEATED HIS THREE opponents in the presidential election with 40 percent of the vote. Southern leaders feared that Lincoln would take away their rights to make their own laws, especially those that protected slavery. They had threatened to **secede** from the Union if he was elected.

South Carolina was the first state to make good on that threat. It seceded on December 20, 1860, six weeks after Lincoln's election. Over the next month, six other Southern states (Mississippi, Florida, Alabama, Georgia, Louisiana, and Texas) left the Union. Before Lincoln's **inauguration**, these states' leaders met to establish their own independent nation, the Confederate States of America. They chose **Jefferson Davis** of Mississippi as their president. Within months, they were joined by Virginia, Arkansas, Tennessee, and North Carolina. The "border states" of Delaware, Maryland, Kentucky, and Missouri, while still slave states, remained in the Union. This situation caused a lot of political tension.

As Lincoln began his first term as president, the nation was divided in two and on the brink of war.

Jefferson Davis was the first and only president of the Confederate States of America.

Charleston

Charleston Harbor

☆ *Fort Sumter*

SOUTH CAROLINA

ATLANTIC OCEAN

1 MILE
(1.6 kilometers)

CHAPTER 5

FORT SUMTER

The commander of a U.S. fort in
South Carolina refused to surrender to
Confederate forces. His decision sparked
the opening shots of the Civil War.

AS EACH STATE SECEDED, IT SEIZED ALL Union properties within its borders. Most U.S. military bases surrendered without resistance. But Major Robert Anderson refused to give up his command at Fort Moultrie in Charleston, South Carolina. Instead he moved his troops to nearby Fort Sumter, which was easier to defend from attack.

As the fort was running out of supplies, Anderson asked for help from the federal government. Lincoln sent a supply ship, but the Confederates were determined to take the fort before the ship arrived. At 4:30 a.m. on Friday, April 12, 1861, Confederate rockets lit up the sky over Fort Sumter. It was soon shrouded in the smoke of exploding missiles. Anderson held out for 34 hours under a continuous bombardment before finally surrendering. The flag of the United States was lowered, and the Confederate flag was raised over the fort.

The Confederates had committed an act of war that Lincoln could not ignore. Two days later, he called for 75,000 volunteers to take up arms and ordered a **blockade** of Southern ports. The American Civil War had begun.

A Confederate flag flies above Fort Sumter after the battle in April 1861.

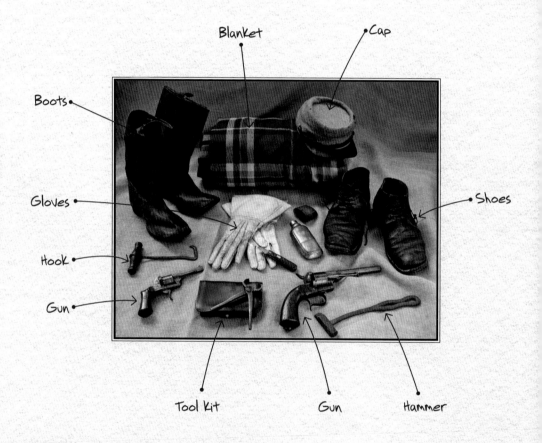

Civil War soldiers carried a variety of items into battle.

CHAPTER 6

RAW RECRUITS

Most soldiers went off to war not knowing
much about fighting or firearms, but
they didn't let that stop them.

AT THE START OF THE WAR, FEW SOLDIERS on either side had ever seen combat. The last time the nation had been at war was the Mexican War (1846–48), 13 years earlier. New volunteers were trained how to fire their Springfield rifles and march in formation. Recruits on both sides didn't like military discipline and rules. They often took breaks when they felt like it and refused to obey orders. And though they were ready to shoot their enemies, they also realized that these enemies were fellow Americans. The two sides came up with nicknames for each other. Northern soldiers called their opponents Johnny Rebs (for Rebels), and Southerners referred to Northern soldiers as Billy Yanks (for Yankees) or just Yanks.

Soldiers who fought in the Civil War were often very young. The average age of Union soldiers was just under 26, and Confederates were probably younger. Many soldiers were under age 18, and some may have been as young as 11. Too small to handle a rifle, these child soldiers beat the drums as their older comrades marched into battle.

A Union drummer boy in 1863

JULY 21

*Confederate forces
win the Battle of Bull
Run near Manassas,
Virginia, in the South.*

1861 JAN FEB MAR APR MAY JUN JUL AUG SEP

CHAPTER 7

THE FIRST BATTLE OF THE WAR

Many Northerners thought they would easily defeat the Southerners in the Battle of Bull Run, but they were in for a rude awakening.

THE FIRST FEW MONTHS OF THE WAR SAW no major fighting. Then, on July 21, 1861, 30,000 Union soldiers marched 25 miles (40 kilometers) from Washington, D.C., to Manassas, Virginia. There, near a stream called Bull Run, they were met by a Confederate army of 34,000.

Hundreds of well-dressed men and women rode out from Washington, D.C., in carriages and buggies to watch the Confederates go down in defeat. They sat atop hills overlooking the battlefield, picnicking and watching the fight as if it were entertainment. The show, however, did not have the ending they expected. It was the Union army that was sent running after a strong Confederate counterattack. The panicking spectators rushed to their carriages and hurried back to Washington.

Each army suffered about 2,000 **casualties**. The Battle of Bull Run showed the North that the South would not be beaten easily. People now knew that the war would be a long, difficult fight.

In the South, this battle is known as the Battle of Manassas. The Union often named battles after the nearest body of water, while the Confederacy named them after the nearest town.

Union army soldiers practice firing a cannon in a drill in Virginia.

" *I can anticipate no greater calamity for the country than a dissolution of the Union.* **"**

—Robert E. Lee, 1861

CHAPTER 8

CONFEDERATE GENERALS

The South's greatest generals were
renowned for their leadership.

THE UNION RECOGNIZED THE GREATNESS of **Robert E. Lee** as a military leader at the war's outbreak. Lincoln offered him command of the Union army, but Lee refused the position. Instead, he remained loyal to his home state of Virginia in the South. There, President Jefferson Davis offered him command of the Army of Northern Virginia in 1862. Lee accepted.

For the next three years, his strategic skills resulted in victory after victory, keeping Southern hopes alive. Lee forced a Northern army of 100,000 to retreat from an attack on Richmond, the Confederate capital. Then he oversaw a second Southern victory at Bull Run, working side by side with **Thomas "Stonewall" Jackson**, another brilliant general.

Lee was a fierce warrior in battle, but off the field he was a gentleman, well-liked by almost everyone who knew him.

General Robert E. Lee (center)
in Richmond, Virginia, in 1865

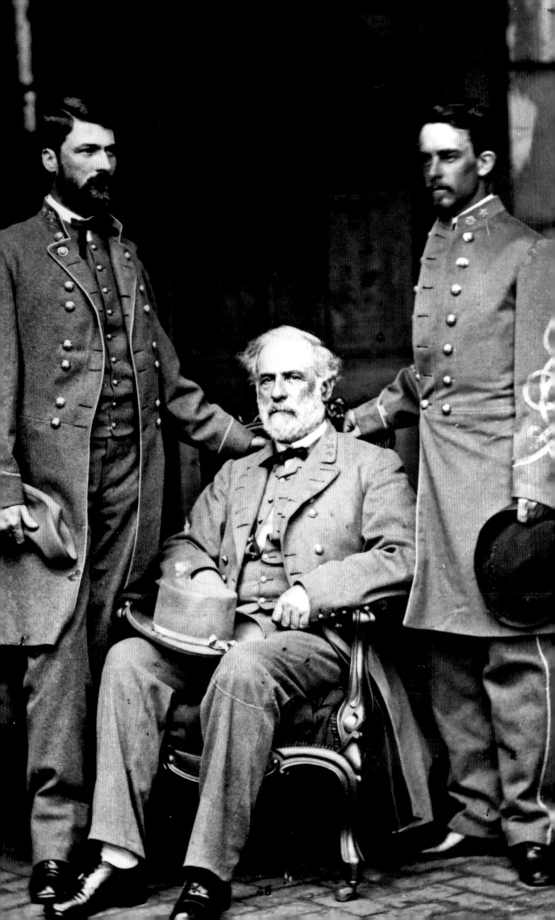

A cap worn by Union soldiers during the war

CHAPTER 9

UNION GENERALS

Lincoln had bad luck choosing his top generals,
and the North paid dearly for it.

WHILE THE SOUTH HAD A SOLID military leader in Lee, President Lincoln had a difficult time finding the right general to head the main Union army, called the Army of the Potomac. His first choice, **George McClellan**, was a superb organizer of troops and a brilliant tactician. However, he often avoided leading his army into battle because he did not want to risk losing men.

Frustrated by McClellan's behavior, Lincoln recalled him in March 1862 and tried several other generals in the position. But each had his own failings. In desperation, Lincoln put McClellan back in charge in August.

The Union general met Lee's army at Sharpsburg, Maryland, near Antietam Creek, in September 1862. The Battle of Antietam resulted in the <u>bloodiest single day of the war</u>. The Union won the battle, but McClellan didn't pursue Lee and his troops as they fled in defeat. He allowed them to escape when he might have ended the war. Lincoln was furious. In November 1862, he relieved McClellan of command for the last time.

About 23,100 soldiers were killed, wounded, or went missing.

President Lincoln (center) meets with Major Alan Pinkerton (left) and a Union general at a Union camp in Maryland in 1862.

These two nearly identical photographs of a Confederate ironclad ship are a stereograph. They were paired to produce the illusion of a single 3D image when viewed through a stereoscope.

CHAPTER 10

THE "MONITOR" AND THE "MERRIMACK"

The showdown between these incredible ships opened a new era in naval warfare.

ON MARCH 8, 1862, A STRANGE-LOOKING SHIP sailed out of Virginia's Norfolk Harbor. It was covered in metal armor, an "ironclad" like no other ship before it. This Confederate vessel was officially named the *Virginia* but was also known as the *Merrimack*. It terrorized the crews of Union **frigates** blocking the entrance of Norfolk Harbor to keep Confederate supplies from coming in.

The *Merrimack* damaged or sank several Union ships that day. But when it returned the following day to finish off the remaining ships, its path was blocked by a ship that looked even stranger: the USS *Monitor*, a Union gunboat that was similarly clad in metal armor. For about four hours, the two ironclads blasted each other, with no clear winner. Then the *Merrimack* sprung a leak and retreated.

It never fought again. The Confederates burned and sank it when they evacuated Norfolk. The *Monitor* barely outlasted the *Merrmack*. Sailing south, it went down in a storm off the coast of North Carolina.

Despite their short lives, the ironclads were not forgotten. Metal ships would soon completely replace wooden ones in the world's navies.

Officers pose on the deck of the USS Monitor.

The first page of President Lincoln's handwritten original Emancipation Proclamation

CHAPTER 11

THE EMANCIPATION PROCLAMATION

Lincoln's historic proclamation freed no slaves,
but it made the Civil War a battle of morals.

ON SEPTEMBER 22, 1862, PRESIDENT Abraham Lincoln made one of the major decisions of the war. In the Emancipation Proclamation, he announced that "all persons held as slaves within any State . . . in rebellion against the United States shall be then, thenceforward, and forever free" as of January 1, 1863. Up until then, Lincoln had been willing to allow slavery to continue in the South if it would preserve the Union. Now he saw that bolder measures had to be taken to defeat the Confederacy.

Ironically, his Emancipation Proclamation freed not a single slave. The Confederacy wasn't about to follow the Union's orders and release its slaves. No slaves were freed in the border states, either. However, the Emancipation Proclamation had other effects. It injected spirit and energy into the Union's cause and increased its stature around the world. It also encouraged ex-slaves and free black men to join the Union army, something Lincoln's generals had wanted for some time.

An enslaved family in South Carolina poses for a photo in 1862.

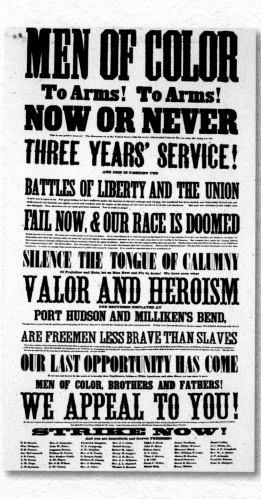

A recruitment poster encourages black men to join the Union army.

CHAPTER 12

BLACK SOLDIERS

Some black soldiers got the opportunity to fight
for the Union. Many of them became heroes.

WHEN THE WAR STARTED, MANY African Americans were eager to join the Union army to prove their patriotism and help end slavery. But the government was afraid that white soldiers wouldn't fight alongside black men or even be part of the same army.

This changed with the announcement of the Emancipation Proclamation and the new perception of the war as a moral struggle to end slavery. In addition, the Union army was in desperate need of recruits. By the end of the war in 1865, there were about 180,000 black men in the Union army. Most of them were limited to **garrison** duty or manual labor. Some, however, saw combat.

One of the most distinguished black **regiments** was the 54th Massachusetts Infantry. On July 18, 1863, members of the 54th stormed Fort Wagner in South Carolina as part of a larger force. Outnumbered by the fort's defenders, nearly half of them were killed, wounded, or captured. These black soldiers faced death bravely, and their regiment brothers continued to fight with distinction in South Carolina, Georgia, and Florida for the remainder of the war.

The story of the 54th Infantry was made into a popular movie, Glory, in 1989.

Black soldiers of the 107th Infantry in 1863

Cannons were a key part of Civil War battles.

CHAPTER 13

THE BATTLE OF CHANCELLORSVILLE

This battle was a big victory for the South,
but also one of its darkest days.

ON MAY 1, 1863, CONFEDERATE GENERAL Lee's army met the Union army led by General Joseph Hooker at Chancellorsville, Virginia. Lee's troops were outnumbered almost two to one, but he designed a bold plan of attack and split his forces in two. During the battle, the forces split again. One group, led by Stonewall Jackson, sneaked around the Union army and made a surprise attack, forcing Hooker to retreat. It was a brilliant strategy and the high point of Lee's military career. But it had an unexpected ending.

On the evening of May 2, Jackson and his men were out scouting the area until dark. As they returned to camp, their fellow soldiers mistook them for the enemy and opened fire. Jackson was seriously wounded, and his left arm had to be **amputated**. When Lee heard the news, he lamented, "He has lost his left arm, but I have lost my right arm [Jackson]." Despite efforts to save his life, Jackson died eight days later.

One in 13 Civil War veterans became amputees due to their injuries.

Wounded Union soldiers rest after the Battle of Chancellorsville in May 1863.

> 66 *War loves to come like a thief in the night.* 99

—AMBROSE BIERCE

CHAPTER 14

THE WAR IN LITERATURE

The stories of Civil War veterans
revealed the horrors of combat.

THE MOST FAMOUS NOVEL OF THE CIVIL War, Stephen Crane's _The Red Badge of Courage_, was published in 1895. Born six years after the war ended, Crane conducted interviews with Civil War veterans to give his book authentic details.

Civil War soldiers sometimes wrote about their experiences as well. The most famous was Ambrose Bierce of Indiana, who fought bravely for the Union and was wounded at the Battle of Kennesaw Mountain in Georgia. Bierce's short stories about the Civil War are filled with bitterness and irony. In one story, a soldier discovers that an enemy he has killed is his brother. In another, a Southern spy imagines his escape as he is about to be hanged. While he came to hate war, Bierce had mixed feelings about his war service. "I never hear a rifle-shot without a thrill in my veins," he wrote.

Crane based the central battle in his novel on the Battle of Chancellorsville.

Writer and Civil War veteran Ambrose Bierce in 1900

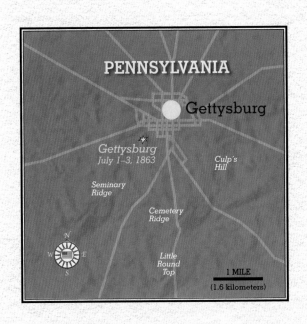

PENNSYLVANIA

Gettysburg

Gettysburg
July 1–3, 1863

Culp's
Hill

Seminary
Ridge

Cemetery
Ridge

N
W · E
S

Little
Round
Top

1 MILE
(1.6 kilometers)

CHAPTER 15

THE BATTLE OF GETTYSBURG

It was the longest and bloodiest battle
ever fought in the Western Hemisphere,
and it cost both sides dearly.

ENCOURAGED BY HIS VICTORY AT Chancellorsville, Confederate general Lee decided to invade the North. On July 1, 1863, he arrived at the town of Gettysburg in southern Pennsylvania. There, his army of about 75,000 faced 90,000 Union troops led by General George Meade in the Battle of Gettysburg.

The battle raged for three days. Then, on July 3, the Confederates made a daring assault on Cemetery Ridge, held firmly by Union soldiers. The 15,000 Confederate soldiers had to scramble across 1 mile (1.6 km) of open ground in the face of direct fire to reach the ridge. Although they came close, they never made it to the top.

It was a doomed effort and a turning point in the battle. With nearly a third of his army gone, Lee had no choice but to retreat back to the South. Meade's army was too weary to pursue him. Lee had survived the Battle of Gettysburg, but never again would he invade Northern territory.

The combined number of casualties at Gettysburg may have been as high as 50,000.

Soldiers gather near a Union hospital tent during the Battle of Gettysburg in 1863.

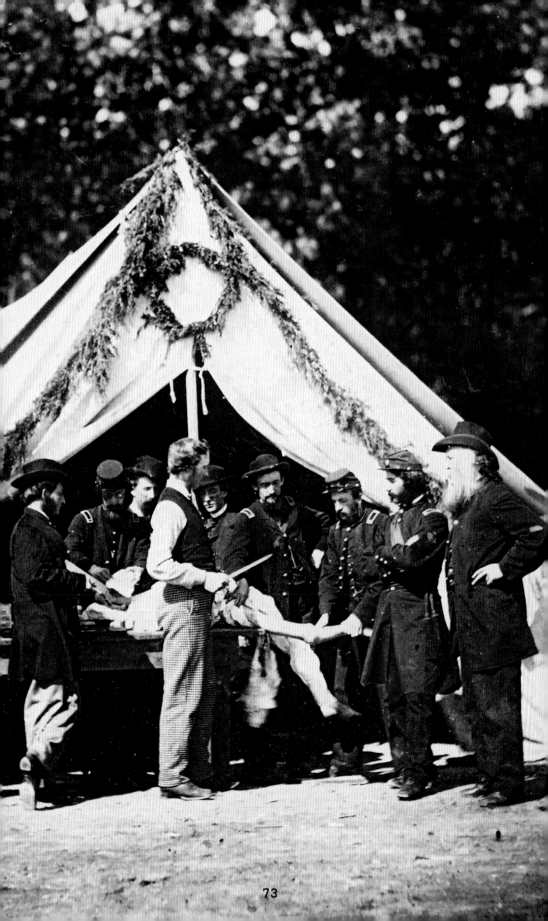

JULY 13–17

At least 100 people are killed in the New York City draft riots.

1863 JAN FEB MAR APR MAY JUN JUL AUG SEP

CHAPTER 16

THE DRAFT RIOTS

It was the worst violence
New York City had ever seen.

A T ALMOST THE SAME TIME AS ITS VICTORY at Gettysburg in July 1863, the Union captured Vicksburg, Mississippi, a key port that gave it control of the Mississippi River. However, celebrations in the North were marred by the worst civilian violence of the war.

With the enlistment of army volunteers lagging, Congress had passed the Union **Conscription** Act in March 1863. This law required men to join the armed services. The only way out of the **draft** was to pay the government $300. Many working-class men didn't have the money to avoid the draft, and the unfairness angered them. In New York City, that anger boiled over into riots that lasted five days in the summer heat. Houses and stores were looted and burned. At least 100 people were killed or wounded, including a number of innocent black people who were blamed for the war and for taking jobs from poor whites. It took 13 regiments of soldiers rushing to the city fresh from Gettysburg to put down the riots. To calm the situation and bring peace, city officials agreed to pay the $300 for any man who did not want to be drafted.

A mob burned the Colored Orphan Asylum in Manhattan, and 233 orphaned black children barely escaped with their lives.

A Union officer chooses names from a lottery box to determine who will be drafted in 1863.

*Union army soldiers pose with
a cannon in June 1862.*

CHAPTER 17

GENERAL ULYSSES S. GRANT

Lincoln finally found a brilliant general for his troops: future U.S. president Ulysses S. Grant.

Grant's fame as a general would later win him the presidency. He served two terms, from 1869 to 1877.

ON MARCH 9, 1864, PRESIDENT LINCOLN appointed **Ulysses S. Grant** <u>commander in chief</u> of all the Union armies. It was a surprising choice in some ways. Grant had been an average student at West Point, the military academy in New York, but excelled in horsemanship. He served bravely in the Mexican War, but later resigned from the army to go into business. He failed as a farmer and as a shopkeeper.

It was his love for the Union that led him to return to the army when the Civil War began. Grant immediately became a top officer in the Union army at the start of the war, but not everyone thought he was well suited to the job. Critics demanded that the president replace him, but Lincoln replied, "I can't spare this man. He fights." Grant proved himself a fighter and a winner in victories at Vicksburg, Mississippi, and Chattanooga, Tennessee. His stubbornness in engaging the enemy earned him the nickname Unconditional Surrender Grant. In Grant, Confederate general Robert E. Lee had finally met his match.

General Ulysses S. Grant stands near his headquarters in Virginia in 1864.

66 *This nation, under God, shall have a new birth of freedom—and that government of the people, by the people, for the people, shall not perish from the earth.* 99

—FINAL WORDS OF ABRAHAM LINCOLN'S
GETTYSBURG ADDRESS, NOVEMBER 1863

CHAPTER 18

LINCOLN'S GETTYSBURG ADDRESS

Just 272 words long, the Gettysburg Address is considered one of the greatest speeches in American history.

ON NOVEMBER 19, 1863, MORE THAN FOUR months after the Battle of Gettysburg, a 17-acre (6.9-hectare) cemetery for fallen soldiers was dedicated at the site. Famed **orator** Edward Everett gave a two-hour speech at the dedication. He was followed by President Lincoln, who was asked to make a few brief remarks. Lincoln's short speech was over before a photographer could adjust his camera to take his picture. The president was not happy with how it went. He later whispered to an aide, "That speech went sour." But the next day, Everett told Lincoln that he wished he had done as well in two hours as the president had in two minutes.

Over the years, the Gettysburg Address has come to be seen as one of the greatest expressions, in simple and clear language, of the ideals that the United States stands for. Lincoln told the world that the Civil War was fought not only to free the slaves and unify a divided nation but to preserve the ideals of freedom and liberty that still define America today.

This is believed to be the only photograph of President Lincoln taken at Gettysburg on the day of his famous speech.

President Lincoln

" *I thread my way through the hospital,*
The hurt and wounded I pacify with soothing hand,
I sit by the restless all the dark night,
   some are so young,
Some suffer so much . . . "

—EXCERPT FROM "THE WOUND-DRESSER,"
AN 1867 POEM BY WALT WHITMAN

CHAPTER 19

ANGELS OF THE BATTLEFIELD

Nurses played a vital role in the Civil War.

Not all Civil War nurses were women. Poet Walt Whitman was among the men who volunteered to work in military hospitals in Washington.

↑

DURING THE CIVIL WAR, <u>WOMEN</u> DID NOT fight in battles. However, they played a major role as nurses, helping thousands of wounded and sick soldiers.

Clara Barton, a 33-year-old woman from New England, moved to Washington, D.C., in 1854 to work in the U.S. Patent Office. When the war broke out, she tended to wounded soldiers who returned to the capital. Barton organized other women as nurses in Washington hospitals, but received no help or encouragement from the government or the military. This didn't stop her from traveling to the front lines to nurse injured soldiers. "I went in while the battle raged," she said proudly. Grateful wounded soldiers called Barton the "Angel of the Battlefield." After the war, she helped establish an American branch of the International Red Cross, a charity that today focuses on disaster relief.

Many of the wounded and sick didn't have the luxury of going to hospitals. They returned to their homes to be cared for by their family members. Some volunteer nurses in the South took wounded soldiers into their own homes to care for them.

A nurse prepares to spoon-feed a wounded soldier in Pennsylvania in 1861.

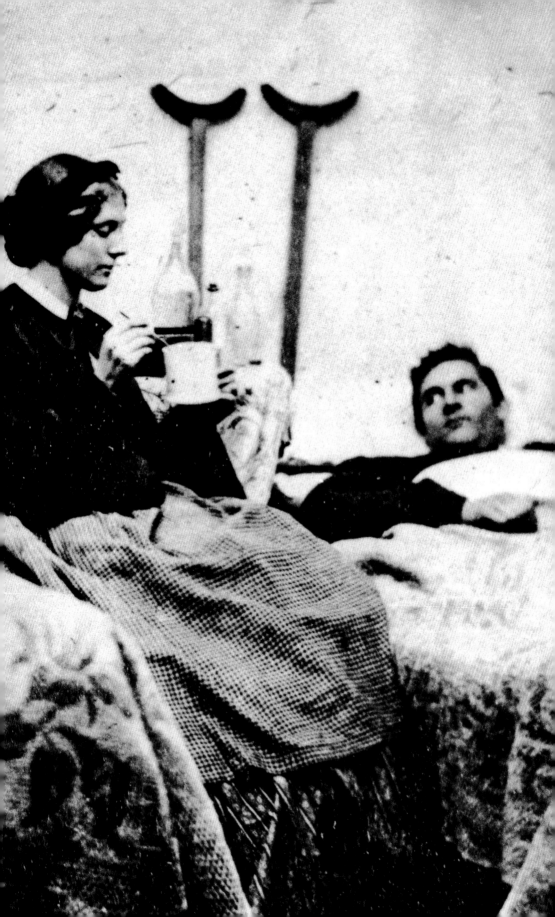

A Union soldier with his rifle

CHAPTER 20

STAYING IN TOUCH

The only thing that gave a soldier more joy than
writing a letter home was receiving one.

TO KEEP IN TOUCH WITH PEOPLE BACK home, Civil War soldiers often wrote letters and kept journals and diaries. They wrote to parents, friends, wives, and girlfriends. They wrote about the fighting they saw, life in camp, and how much they missed family and friends. "Oh how I long to see them once more," Confederate infantryman Henry Allen of Virginia wrote to his wife about their children. "Kiss them for me and tell them I expect to find them good children." Mothers and wives not only wrote back but sometimes sent home-cooked foods in packages that were eagerly awaited by their soldiers. Knowing how important mail was to soldiers, the Union army set up post offices near almost every fort and camp. By 1864, a soldier could mail his letters for free as long as he wrote "Soldier's Letter" on the envelope.

Confederate soldiers had a tougher time with their correspondence. Shortages of paper, stamps, and envelopes posed a challenge. "Excuse my writing with pencil, as ink is scarce in camp," wrote one Texas soldier to his father.

Union soldiers write letters and mend clothing during downtime between battles in the early 1860s.

Many of these letters were passed down through families and now reside in archives and libraries, offering an invaluable picture of the war from the soldiers' viewpoint.

*A Union officer says good-bye
to his wife before heading
off to fight in the war.*

CHAPTER 21

THE HOME FRONT— NORTH AND SOUTH

The war changed everyday life in both the North and the South.

WHILE UNION SOLDIERS FACED HARDSHIPS on the battlefield, the economy back home was doing very well. War created a tremendous demand for goods and foods in the North. New factories sprang up, and people went to work making **munitions**, clothing, iron, and steel. Farmers kept busy producing grains and vegetables to feed the soldiers.

But not everyone in the North was happy. Many Southern sympathizers in the North were arrested and put in prison without trial. President Lincoln argued that the dangers of war demanded such actions.

It was a very different picture in the South. A largely agricultural society, the South had little industry, and most of its manufactured goods had come from the North or abroad. Once at war, the North supplied nothing to its enemy. Northern warships also set up blockades outside Southern ports to prevent ships from bringing goods from Europe. By the war's end, Southerners were making clothes out of carpets and curtains and eating whatever food they grew that Union soldiers hadn't destroyed.

They were called "Copperheads," after a poisonous snake. Generally, they were politicians and newspaper editors.

A woman operates a sewing machine around 1860.

MISSISSIPPI RIVER

MISSISSIPPI

ALABAMA

LOUISIANA

FLORIDA

New Orleans

Mobile

Mobile Bay

GULF OF MEXICO

N
W E
S

40 MILES
(64 kilometers)

CHAPTER 22

"DAMN THE TORPEDOES! FULL SPEED AHEAD!"

Mobile Bay was lined with mines that could blow up a ship, but that didn't stop Union admiral David Farragut.

BY THE SUMMER OF 1864, UNION FORCES HAD closed every Confederate port on the Gulf of Mexico but one—Mobile, Alabama. This made it even more challenging for the South to import needed food and supplies from abroad. Closing off the last port would cut off the South's supplies completely. The bay was guarded by two forts and a string of mines, then called torpedoes, that could sink an enemy ship.

Despite the port's protection, Union rear admiral David Farragut was not discouraged. On the morning of August 5, 1864, he led his fleet of Union ships into Mobile Bay. One Union ironclad was struck by a torpedo and sunk. The rest of the ships hesitated to continue until Farragut leaped onto his ship's rigging and cried, "Damn the torpedoes! Full speed ahead!" The fleet charged into the bay, and after a three-hour battle the Union emerged victorious. Farragut, at age 63, became a national hero.

Farragut became a naval seaman at age 9 and fought in his first battle at age 13, during the War of 1812.

Admiral David Farragut in 1863

NOVEMBER 8

*Lincoln is elected
to a second term
as president.*

MAY JUN JUL AUG SEP OCT NOV DEC **1865**

CHAPTER 23

THE ELECTION OF 1864

President Lincoln's chances of re-election looked slim until the fortunes of war suddenly changed.

The United States became the first nation in history to hold a general election during a major war.

SOME NORTHERNERS WANTED TO POSTPONE the presidential election while the war was going on, but President <u>Lincoln refused to do so.</u> However, it seemed doubtful he would be reelected. Most efforts of the North in the spring and summer of 1864 were producing little results. Meanwhile, Union General **William T. Sherman** was waging a long and frustrating **siege** of Atlanta, Georgia. Union casualties were rising, and many people blamed Lincoln for the deaths of so many soldiers.

As the elections approached, the Democrats in the North wanted to negotiate a peace settlement with the Confederacy. They nominated George McClellan to <u>run against Lincoln</u> for president. Then suddenly, after months of fighting, Sherman finally took Atlanta on September 2. Around the same time, Grant pushed his army toward Petersburg, Virginia. It was clear the North was winning the war, and Lincoln's policies had been validated. On Election Day, November 8, Lincoln won in a landslide.

In 1864, newspaper editor Horace Greeley said about the president: "Mr. Lincoln is already beaten. He cannot be elected." He was wrong.

General Sherman's troops use wheelbarrows to transport cannonballs in 1864.

Cannonballs were made of heavy metal.

TENNESSEE

SOUTH
CAROLINA

Atlanta

ALABAMA

GEORGIA

Savannah

ATLANTIC
OCEAN

N
W E
S

FLORIDA

GULF OF MEXICO

40 MILES
(64 kilometers)

CHAPTER 24

SHERMAN'S MARCH TO THE SEA

Union general William Sherman waged
total war on the South in his famous march,
changing the nature of warfare forever.

AFTER TAKING ATLANTA, SHERMAN HEADED east with his 60,000-man army. His goal was the city of Savannah near the Atlantic coast. Over the course of five weeks on his 285-mile (459 km) "March to the Sea," Sherman destroyed nearly everything in his path. He ordered his troops to burn homes, barns, and fields. They tore up railroad tracks and cut telegraph wires. The purpose was to destroy the South's remaining resources and its will to fight. By waging total war against civilians in the countryside, Sherman hoped to bring the war to a quick end and ultimately save lives.

The Southerners who suffered from his march hated Sherman with a passion. Northerners, however, hailed him as a hero after he arrived in Savannah on December 21. That day, Sherman sent a message to Lincoln: "I beg to present you as a Christmas gift the City of Savannah, with one hundred and fifty guns and plenty of ammunition, also about twenty-five thousand bales of cotton."

General Sherman shortly before leading his men into Atlanta

" *The war began in my front yard and ended in my parlor [living room].* **"**

—WILMER MCLEAN,
A CIVILIAN AFFECTED BY THE WAR

CHAPTER 25

BATTLES IN THE BACKYARD

For many civilians, especially in the South, the war got a lot closer than they would have liked.

THE CIVIL WAR WAS UP CLOSE AND personal for many civilians long before Sherman cut his way across the state of Georgia. Battlefields were often next to farms and homes. Military leaders often **commandeered** a home and used it as a headquarters before or during a battle. One of the many families whose homes were commandeered during the war was the Carter family of Franklin, Tennessee, in the South. Their home was taken over by Union officers during the Battle of Franklin in November 1864. The family huddled in a room as 60,000 soldiers fought fiercely through the night. The next morning, they went outside to find their yard filled with dead soldiers.

The war also threatened civilian lives. Twenty-year-old Jennie Wade was baking biscuits in her kitchen during the Battle of Gettysburg in 1863 when she was struck and killed by a sharpshooter's bullet through a window. These are just two examples of battles that affected civilians during the Civil War. There were many more.

The bodies of dead soldiers lay in front of a farmhouse after the Battle of Antietam in Maryland in 1862.

APRIL 9

Lee surrenders to Grant at
Appomattox Court House
in Virginia, effectively
ending the war.

1865 JAN FEB MAR APR MAY JUN JUL AUG

CHAPTER 26

SURRENDER
AT APPOMATTOX

The war had been violent and bloody,
but the final surrender was
handled with grace and dignity.

BY THE START OF APRIL 1865, GRANT HAD taken Petersburg, Virginia, and was laying siege to Richmond, Virginia, the Confederate capital. When he seized the city's only railroad, it cut off supplies coming in to Lee and his army. Lee retreated, but Grant quickly caught up with him. Realizing that further fighting would mean a useless sacrifice of lives, Lee sent a message to Grant asking for a meeting to discuss terms of surrender.

On Sunday, April 9, 1865, the two generals met in Wilmer McLean's farmhouse in Appomattox Court House in Virginia. Grant arrived dressed in a dirty private's coat. Lee, dressed in a clean gray uniform, looked more like the victor. Grant was generous in his conditions. All of the Confederate soldiers could go home. They could keep their horses for spring plowing, and the officers could keep their pistols. Grant didn't want Union soldiers to celebrate the war's end. "The Confederates were now our prisoners, and we did not want to exult on their downfall," he later said. Few soldiers, however, followed his command. The war was over, and they were filled with joy.

Union soldiers pose in front of Appomattox Court House.

This small pistol was used to kill President Lincoln.

CHAPTER 27

THE PRESIDENT HAS BEEN SHOT!

In the midst of the Union triumph, the nation
would undergo still one more tragedy.

PRESIDENT LINCOLN WAS INAUGURATED for the second time in March 1865, a month before the end of the war. In his inaugural address, he called for a peace between North and South "with **malice** towards none, with charity for all." But malice was still alive in the land, especially among some Southerners and those who sympathized with them.

Just five days after Lee's surrender, on the evening of April 14, 1865, the president attended a play at Ford's Theatre in Washington. Just after 10 p.m., actor John Wilkes Booth quietly entered the presidential box and fired one bullet into the back of Lincoln's head. Booth, a Southern sympathizer who hated Lincoln, fled the theater. Lincoln was carried across the street to a boardinghouse where he died the next morning. Booth fled to Virginia, where he was found and killed by federal troops 12 days later. Lincoln's death was mourned across the nation, even by many Southerners. Many historians believe that if he had lived, he would have helped to heal the nation's wounds and would have brought the South back into the Union with dignity and compassion.

John Wilkes Booth in 1865

*Captured Confederate cannons
in Richmond, Virginia, in 1865*

CHAPTER 28

THE ASHES OF WAR

The Civil War caused much suffering, but it also made the United States stronger.

THE CIVIL WAR REMAINS THE COSTLIEST conflict that the United States has ever fought. Around 690,000 people—soldiers and civilians—died. Another half million were wounded, some of whom were permanently maimed. The economic cost to the North was more than $3 billion. To the South, it was also nearly $3 billion. However, the South, where most of the fighting took place, was the more devastated. Many of its cities and towns had been leveled, and its countryside was scarred. The war left a bitterness and hatred on both sides that would take generations to heal.

But good did come out of the agony of war. Slavery was officially ended, and four million African Americans would soon become free citizens. War boosted manufacturing in the North, providing jobs and improving the lives of millions of people. As for the country itself, it had faced the ultimate test of its unity and had emerged whole. The United States would go on to become the world's leading democracy and a beacon of freedom to the world.

Children sit among destroyed buildings in Charleston, South Carolina, in 1865.

*Andrew Johnson of Tennessee served
as president from 1865 to 1869.*

CHAPTER 29

RECONSTRUCTION

After the war, it was time to rebuild
and heal the damaged nation.

PRESIDENT LINCOLN WANTED THE POSTWAR period of Reconstruction (1866–77) to be one of forgiveness and healing for the South. His successor, **Andrew Johnson**, tried to continue Lincoln's policies. But as a Southerner he was viewed with suspicion by Northerners in Congress. They wanted to punish the Southern states for going to war against the Union and called for Johnson's **impeachment** and removal from office. While he was impeached in the House of Representatives, the Senate failed to convict him by one vote. Johnson's presidency was saved but seriously weakened.

A group of politicians called the Radical Republicans took control of Reconstruction and put the Southern states under military rule. Former Confederate officials were denied voting rights and could not run for political office.

However, some steps toward equality were made during Reconstruction. In many places, black men, now full citizens, were elected to state offices for the first time and fulfilled their duties admirably. By 1870, all 11 Confederate states were reorganized and readmitted to the Union.

In 1866, two men sit near a church in Charleston, South Carolina, that is beir repaired after being damaged in the wa

66 *Neither slavery nor involuntary servitude . . . shall exist within the United States, or any place subject to their jurisdiction.* **99**

—THE 13TH AMENDMENT TO THE U.S. CONSTITUTION, 1865

CHAPTER 30

CIVIL RIGHTS AND WRONGS

Slavery had ended in the United States, but
prejudice and racism were still alive.

THE ABOLITION OF SLAVERY WAS COMPLETED with the passing of the 13th **Amendment** to the U.S. Constitution in December 1865. Two more amendments **ratified** by the states over the next five years gave African Americans full civil rights. The 14th Amendment made former slaves American citizens, and the 15th Amendment gave them the right to vote. For a few years, black people enjoyed these constitutional rights. But as Southern states were readmitted to the Union and regained control of their governments, things changed. Many white Southerners continued to treat black people as inferior. They passed laws making it extremely difficult, if not impossible, for black people to vote. They also passed what were known as Jim Crow laws, which **segregated** black people and treated them unjustly.

It would take another hundred years before the modern civil rights movement finally earned African Americans the opportunities that they were promised in 1865.

They were named for a character used to make fun of black people in the South in the 1800s

The cover of an 1867 issue of Harper's Weekly *reports on African Americans casting votes for the first time.*

HARPER'S WEEKLY.

A JOURNAL OF CIVILIZATION

XI.—No. 568.]   NEW YORK, SATURDAY, NOVEMBER 16, 1867.   [SINGLE COPIES TEN CENTS.
[$4.00 PER YEAR IN ADVANCE.

Entered according to Act of Congress, in the Year 1867, by Harper & Brothers, in the Clerk's Office of the District Court for the Southern District of New York.

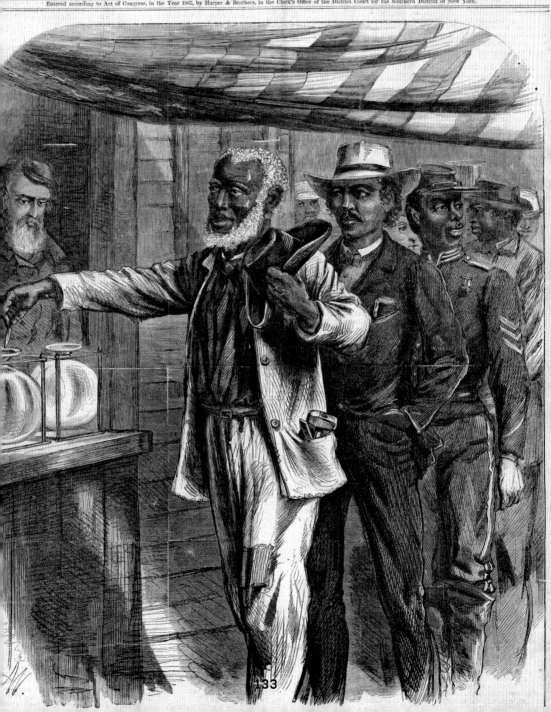

KEY PLAYERS

 **President Abraham Lincoln** (1861–65) was elected as the nation was facing its greatest crisis since its founding. His determination to keep the United States as one nation helped make him one of the country's greatest presidents.

 **President Andrew Johnson** (1865–69) was thrust into the presidency upon Lincoln's assassination. While his intentions were good, he lacked Lincoln's political skills and was nearly removed from office in his turbulent time as president.

 **General George McClellan** was commander of the Union Army of the Potomac longer than any other general during the war, but he was a reluctant fighter and was eventually replaced by Ulysses S. Grant.

 **General Ulysses S. Grant** was a dogged fighter who led the Union in victory after victory, often at great sacrifice to his troops. His popularity as a war hero led him to win two terms as president (1869–77) following Johnson's time in office.

General William T. Sherman's stunning capture of Atlanta, Georgia, in 1864 helped Lincoln win a second term as president. His subsequent "March to the Sea" destroyed the resources and morale of the Confederacy.

Confederate president Jefferson Davis had been an outstanding military leader in the Mexican War. But he was a weak and ineffective leader in many ways. At the end of the Civil War, he was imprisoned for treason for two years.

General Robert E. Lee was widely respected as a military commander. In victory after victory, he helped keep the Confederacy alive.

General Stonewall Jackson was the second-greatest Confederate general after Lee and the hero of Bull Run and other battles. His death at the Battle of Chancellorsville was a terrible blow to the Confederacy.

CIVIL WAR TIMELINE

FEBRUARY 4
Seven Southern states establish the Confederate States of America.

OCTOBER 16–18
Abolitionist John Brown's attempt to seize the federal arsenal at Harpers Ferry, Virginia, fails.

NOVEMBER 6
Republican Abraham Lincoln is elected the 16th president of the United States.

OCT NOV DEC **1860** JAN FEB MAR APR MAY JUN JUL AUG SEP OCT **NOV** DEC **1861** JAN **FE**

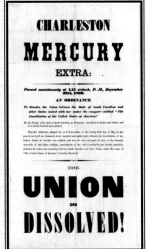

DECEMBER 20
South Carolina becomes the first Southern state to secede from the Union.

MARCH 4
Lincoln takes the oat of office as presiden of a divided nation

APRIL 12
Confederate troops attack Union troops at Fort Sumter in South Carolina, setting off the Civil War.

SEPTEMBER 17
The bloody Battle of Antietam in Maryland ends in a costly Union victory.

APRIL 25
Union warships attack and capture New Orleans, Louisiana, a key Confederate port.

MAY JUN **JUL** AUG SEP OCT NOV DEC **1862** JAN FEB **MAR APR** MAY JUN JUL AUG **SEP** OCT NOV DEC

MARCH 9
The Monitor *and the* Merrimack *fight an indecisive battle near Norfolk Harbor, Virginia.*

JULY 21
Confederate forces ~~w~~in the Battle of Bull ~~R~~un near Manassas, ~~Vir~~ginia, in the South.

JULY 1–3
Union and Confederate troops clash at the Battle of Gettysburg in Pennsylvania.

NOVEMBER 19
Lincoln delivers the Gettysburg Address at the dedication of a new war cemetery.

JANUARY 1
The Emancipation Proclamation takes effect, officially freeing slaves in Confederate states.

1863 JAN FEB **MAR** APR **MAY** JUN **JUL** AUG SEP OCT **NOV** DEC **1864** JAN FEB **MAR** APR

MARCH
The Union Conscription Act passes, beginning a national draft.

JULY 13–17
At least 100 people are killed in the New York City draft riots.

MARCH 9
Lincoln names Ulysses S. Grant commander in chief of all Union armies.

MAY 1–5
Confederate troops led by General Robert E. Lee win the Battle of Chancellorsville in Virginia, but Stonewall Jackson is accidentally shot by his own men and dies eight days later.

AUGUST 5
Union admiral David Farragut wins the Battle of Mobile Bay in Alabama.

NOVEMBER 8
Lincoln is elected to a second term as president.

DECEMBER 21
Sherman captures Savannah, Georgia, after his 285-mile (459 km) march from Atlanta.

APRIL 9
Lee surrenders to Grant at Appomattox Court House in Virginia, effectively ending the war.

JUL **AUG** SEP OCT **NOV** DEC **1865** JAN FEB MAR **APR** MAY JUN JUL AUG SEP OCT NOV DEC

SEPTEMBER 2
Union general William T. Sherman takes Atlanta, Georgia.

APRIL 14
President Lincoln is assassinated by actor John Wilkes Booth at Ford's Theatre in Washington, D.C.

GLOSSARY

- **abolished** (uh-BAH-lisht) put an end to something officially

- **amendment** (uh-MEND-muhnt) a change that is made to a law or a legal document like the Constitution

- **amputated** (AM-pyuh-tay-tid) cut off someone's limb, usually because it is damaged or diseased

- **arsenal** (AHR-suh-nuhl) a place where weapons and ammunition are made or stored

- **blockade** (blah-KADE) the closing off of an area to keep people or supplies from going in or out

- **casualties** (KA-zhul-teez) people who are injured or killed in an accident, a natural disaster, or a war

- **commandeered** (kah-muhn-DEERD) took over for military use

- **conscription** (kuhn-SCRIPT-shuhn) required military service

- **draft** (DRAFT) a system that requires people to serve in the armed forces

- **frigates** (FRIG-utz) large warships

- **garrison** (GAR-uh-suhn) a group of soldiers assigned to defend a town, or the building occupied by these soldiers

- **impeachment** (im-PEECH-muhnt) the process of bringing formal charges against a public official for misconduct

- **inauguration** (in-aw-gyuh-RAY-shuhn) the ceremony of swearing in a public official

- **industrialized** (in-DUHS-tree-uhl-izd) developed to rely more on manufacturing and businesses than farming

- **insurrection** (in-suh-REK-shuhn) violent rebellion

- **malice** (MAL-us) a desire to hurt or embarrass someone

- **munitions** (myoo-NISH-uhnz) military equipment and supplies

- **orator** (OR-uh-tur) someone who is skilled in public speaking

- **ratified** (RAT-uh-fide) agreed to or approved officially

- **regiments** (REJ-uh-muhntz) military units made up of two or more battalions, which are large groups of soldiers

- **secede** (si-SEED) to formally withdraw from a group, organization, or country

- **segregated** (SEG-ri-gay-tid) separated or kept apart from a larger group

- **siege** (SEEJ) the surrounding of a place such as a castle or city to cut off supplies and then wait for those inside to surrender

FIND OUT MORE

BOOKS

Benoit, Peter. *The Surrender at Appomattox.* New York: Children's Press, 2012.

Gregory, Josh. *Gettysburg.* New York: Children's Press, 2012.

Gregory, Josh. *The Gettysburg Address.* New York: Children's Press, 2013.

Raatma, Lucia. *The Underground Railroad.* New York: Children's Press, 2011

VISIT THIS SCHOLASTIC WEB SITE FOR
MORE INFORMATION ABOUT **THE CIVIL WAR**
www.factsfornow.scholastic.com
Enter the keywords **THE CIVIL WAR**

INDEX

Page numbers in *italics* indicate illustrations.

ABOUT THE AUTHOR

Steven Otfinoski has written more than 180 books for young readers. He has written several other books about the Civil War era, including *Yankees and Rebels: Stories of U.S. Civil War Leaders*, *Harriet Tubman and the Underground Railroad*, and *The Story of Juneteenth*. Three of his books have been named to the New York Public Library's list of recommendations, Books for the Teen Age. He lives with his family in Connecticut.